HONESTY OPTIONAL

HONESTY OPTIONAL

KENNETH MULLER

ZOUEV PUBLISHING

This book is printed on acid-free paper.

Copyright © 2016 Kenneth Muller. All rights reserved.

No part of this book may be used or reproduced in any manner whatsoever without written permission, except in the case of brief quotations embodied in critical articles or reviews.

Published 2015
Printed by Lightning Source

ISBN 978-0-9934187-9-2, paperback.

This play is dedicated to those who tell the truth despite the consequences.

Thank you to Lynn Lemaire for her expert editing and advice, to Marleen Van Gyes for coming to see all of my shows and for getting all of the jokes, to Alison Lipp and Neal Dilk for their unwavering support of the arts, to Frank Masanta, Jr. and the gang at the Sun-spring Charity School in Lusaka, Zambia for always inspiring me to do good things, to Frank and Margie Urie for decades of serious laughter, to Brad Masoni (literary genius and buddy extraordinaire) and to Alexander "Sasha" Zouev for getting my words out there.

Synopsis:

Honesty Optional is a contemporary drama/comedy that confronts the blurred lines of honesty and expectations between and among teens and adults. Two very divergent families discover that they have more in common than they might have expected. Everybody cheats at something. Where is the moral compass, and who really has the right to hold it and lead others in the direction it indicates? Community leaders – parents and educators, in this case – find themselves faced with the implications of their own lifestyles and choices.

Playwright, Kenneth Muller, works as an international educator currently teaching and organizing community/global service activities at the American International School of Rotterdam in the Netherlands.

HONESTY OPTIONAL

A Drama/Comedy in Two Acts

By

Kenneth Muller

CAST: 8-20 (minimum of two male players)

Notes:

For this production, we made the bold decision to leave the stage and to go for our own version of theater in the round. In addition, we decided that scenery and props should be kept to a minimum in order to allow the audience to focus on the words, because this is a play about words and the messages they can carry. The success of this production is rooted in the independent work skills of the cast members who, due to scheduling conflicts, had limited opportunities to rehearse together. In spite of the hurdles, the theater experience, yet again, has yielded the actors opportunities to learn more about themselves as well as about the world in which they live.

Cast of Characters

QUINCY JENKINS:

A self-important businessman; husband of DORIS and father of GRACE

DORIS JENKINS:

Wife to QUINCY and mother to GRACE; a frustrated woman approaching middle age, victim of a loveless marriage

GRACE JENKINS:

High-school-aged daughter of QUINCY and DORIS

OWEN MAGEE:

A pleasant and content self-employed man; married to SUZANNE and father of MARLEEN

SUZANNE MAGEE:

Devoted wife to OWEN and supportive mother of MARLEEN

MARLEEN:

A conscientious high school student; daughter of OWEN and SUZANNE

DIRECTOR PETERSON:

Director/superintendent of the local high school attended by GRACE and MARLEEN

PRINCIPAL GUNDERSON:

Principal at the local high school; acutely vacuous

MISS MORRIS:

A dedicated and competent high school teacher

ACTORS 1-8:

These can be assigned to any of the cast members or additional ones if the cast is larger than nine. They deliver the quotes in the prologue.

OPTIONAL ADDITIONS FOR A LARGER CAST

EXAM CLOCK:

Actor costumed as a large clock that circulates the exam room scene and makes ticking sound

BUTLER:

Stands aside during ACT 1, Scene 1 with a bottle of champagne; keeps DORIS'S champagne glass filled

GRANDMOTHER:

Sits in a corner, knitting, during ACT 1, Scene 2; director and cast can create and insert lines for her inclusion in the family discussion

UNDERCOVER POLICE OFFICERS:

Stand on either side of QUINCY during the epilogue; they wear dark suits and sunglasses

PROLOGUE

SETTING: Empty stage

AT RISE: Several cast members stand scattered about the stage. A spot will hit them one at a time as they individually deliver the following poem(s) and quotes.

ACTOR 1
(spot on)
"She may be shaped like an apple or a pear
But this query may be asked in the world out there.
It's not a question you can easily dismiss...
Tell me does my bum look big in this?
She smiles sweetly and awaits your reply...
Tell me guys are you honest - or would you lie!"
Poem by Jan Allison
(spot out)

ACTOR 2
(spot on)
"Occasionally he stumbled over the truth, but hastily picked himself up and hurried on as if nothing had happened." Winston Churchill
(spot out)

ACTOR 3
(spot on)
"Honesty is the best policy – when there is money in it." Mark Twain
(spot out)

ACTOR 4
(spot on)
"Speak the truth, but leave immediately after." A Slovenian proverb.
(spot out)

ACTOR 5
(spot on)
"This above all – to thine own self be true,
And it must follow, as the night the day,
Thou canst not then be false to any man." William Shakespeare
(spot off)

ACTOR 6
(spot on)
"Pretty much all the honest truth telling in the world is done by children." Oliver Wendell Holmes
(spot out)

ACTOR 7
(spot on)
"There are only two ways of telling the complete truth – anonymously and posthumously." Thomas Sowell
(spot out)

ACTOR 8
(spot on)
"The secret of life is honesty and fair dealing. If you can fake that, you've got it made." Groucho Marx
(spot out)

(BLACKOUT)

(END OF SCENE)

ACT I

Scene 1

SETTING: A living room or a simple table with two chairs

AT RISE: QUINCY JENKINS is on the phone, pacing. His wife, DORIS JENKINS, is seated, sipping champagne and skimming through a fashion magazine.

QUINCY
(talking on phone)
Don't question me - I don't have the time or the patience. Just dump the Hallitron stocks and get me one hundred and fifty shares of Servicom.
(a pause while listening to response)
That's not my problem. Just do it!

(puts phone in pocket)

DORIS
(glass of Champagne in hand)
Your charm is only superseded by your patience and genuine warmth for others.

QUINCY
Don't even go there.

DORIS
There are many other places I'd rather go, but those are clearly reserved for your... what is it you call them these days... clients?

QUINCY
Here we go.

DORIS
How does one manage to procure a fleet of curvaceous clients under thirty? Who knew there were so many *Legally Blonde* investors?

QUINCY
Listen, Doris, I give you everything you want - surgeries, shopping sprees, lady lunches and lots of freedom.

DORIS
And I gave you my youth.

QUINCY

Too bad it only lasted as long as a British boy band career.

DORIS
Aren't you clever?
(stands)
Do you really think the perks make up for not having you? For having a for-appearances-only marriage? I have needs too, you know.

QUNICY
We've had this conversation ad nauseum. Why don't you go find yourself a nice toy boy? Cougars are still a thing, right?. All I ask is that you be discreet.

DORIS
I could never do that. It would be humiliating. Besides, if cougars are so "in," why don't you take advantage of the one you have right here instead of parading your mid-life crisis around like it's a medal of honor?

QUINCY
Your gender has more self-control than mine, and THAT is established fact.

DORIS
How convenient for you.

QUNICY
(taking out his phone)
I have to take this.

                    (talking on phone)
OK, in that case, make it two
hundred shares of Servicom.
                    (pauses, listening)
Yes, I'm sure. Nigel promises it'll
be a homerun.
                    (pauses, listening to
                    response on phone)
I am well aware of the legalities
involved, and I'll take my chances.
I don't pay you to be my conscience;
I pay you to take orders. If you
won't do it, Phil or Tom over at E-
Trade will.
                    (pauses for response)
Good then. I want to see the
transaction within the hour.
                    (puts phone in pocket)

                    DORIS
That sounded rather aggressive.

                    QUINCY
Aggressive gets results, darling.
Aggressive pays the Botox and Armani
bills.

                    DORIS
Must you always be so crass?

                    QUINCY
Sorry. Knee-jerk reactions tend to
get the best of me. I'm just all
keyed up about this new investment.
If my broker hesitates because of
some small print about ethics, I...
WE could miss out on making a small
fortune.

DORIS
Is there something **un**ethical about this deal?

QUINCY
The less you know about it, the better.

DORIS
Please don't take any unnecessary risks. We have plenty. In fact, sometimes I think we'd be much happier living a simple life in a trailer in one of the square states.

QUINCY
Really. Sitting on a porch watching leaves drop would kill you just as much as it would kill me.

DORIS
I'm not so sure. There might be fewer distractions for you. We might even stand a chance of becoming a real couple again in a place like that.

QUINCY
You watch too much television. We don't have the DNA for that kind of lifestyle.

DORIS
I don't know. I'm pretty flexible.

QUINCY

Flexible! You can't go one week
without getting some kind of
procedure done. Your face is so
tight, your eyes should be on the
back of your head by now.

               DORIS
Maybe I do that out of boredom.
Maybe pressure.

               QUINCY
I'm not the only one parading a mid-
life crisis around.

               DORIS
Did you ever think that maybe I do
all of this for you? So you'll
notice me as much as you notice your
"clients?"

               QUINCY
Listen, Doris, we make a great team.
You are doing a superb job of
raising Gracie, and we have
everything we need. People envy us.

               DORIS
We do project quite the image, but
sometimes I feel like it's cheating.
People think we're the family of the
century, but really, we're not.

               QUINCY
Aren't we? Look, everyone knows
that relationships evolve. We
married young, our parents approved,
we have a gorgeous, talented
daughter, and we're successful.

DORIS

Financially.

QUINCY

Better than the alternative.

DORIS

I know. I just wish the image we project were something more than an image. I want it to be real.

QUINCY

All families cheat when it comes to projecting images of success and happiness. There is no perfect family, and quite frankly, honesty is overrated.

DORIS

That's depressing.

QUINCY

That's reality.
    (takes out phone)
Good. Keep an eye on the index and by mid-afternoon you will be salivating over the commission that's coming your way. We just kicked some major assets.
    (puts phone in pocket)
It's done.

DORIS
    (a bit defeated)
Yes, I suppose it is.
    (enter GRACE JENKINS,
    their daughter, with some
    textbooks)

Hi, Gracie.

                    QUINCY
Good morning, kiddo. How are the
studies coming along?

                    GRACE
Hi, guys. I'm kinda getting
there... except for the French.

                    QUINCY
The French have always been a pain
in the derrière, so I guess it makes
sense that they'd choose the most
complicated language in Europe for
themselves.

                    DORIS
Nonsense. That's a language that's
easily faked. Just say things like
"vogue," "champagne," "Louis
Vuitton" and C'est la vie." Nobody
will question you.

                    GRACE
Thanks, mom, but the exam is on
subjunctive mood and conditional
verb tenses.

                    QUINCY
               (dismissive)
Subjunctive mood - I think I'm in
one of those. Don't listen to your
mother, Gracie. A language that
requires you to pronounce only half

of the letters in a word is truly
sadistic. I feel for you.
> (takes out his phone and
> looks at it)

Sorry, sweetie, I have to go sign
some papers, have meetings, make
deals - the usual. But I'll see you
at the reception tonight. Bonne
chance. That's French.
> (kisses GRACE on the
> forehead)

Doris, I'll be back to change by
six.

DORIS

Into what? A good husband?
> (delivers a fake laugh)

I'll be here.
> (QUINCY exits)

GRACE

Mom, do I really have to go to that
thing tonight? The exam is first
thing in the morning and I really do
need a few more hours with the
books.

DORIS

Don't be silly, Grace. The
connections you make at functions
with diplomats and quasi-royalty far
outweigh the value of being able to
speak French. I'm sure you know
enough to pass.

GRACE

That may be true, but I don't want
to embarrass myself when I know I

can ace it with just a few more hours of studying.

                  DORIS
Embarrassment is a wasted emotion reserved for the religious and the middle classes. Just let it go. Besides, the Alumni Association has already secured a spot for you at Exeter, so all is good, dear.

                  GRACE
It's not just the exam. Well, mostly it is. I just hate the receptions and parties I get dragged to. Those people are so pretentious and dull.

                  DORIS
Those pretentious, dull people are the ones who make all of the big decisions in this world.

                  GRACE
That explains the pathetic state of it.

                  DORIS
Sarcasm is not your forté. See. More French.

                  GRACE
When I am surrounded by fake people, I have to pretend to be fake too, and I really hate it.

DORIS
Of course you do. Who doesn't? But it is how our world works.

GRACE
That isn't what they teach us at school.

DORIS
(she laughs)
There is an unfathomable chasm of things they don't teach at schools. They aren't allowed to, because reality is not politically correct. Trust me. The more practice you get at being pretentious now, the more easily it will come to you as an adult.

GRACE
Wow. Another parent-of-the-year proverb.

DORIS
Do you think the Kardashians are real? And those hot, young studs who play in those vampire shows you watch? They're not. They go to receptions and put on their best fake just like we do. It yields success. And you worship THEM.

GRACE
Mother, they are celebrities, characters. We aren't.

DORIS
Ah, but we could be. It only takes meeting the right people.... at a

party like the one we are attending tonight!

                GRACE
Really? You want that?

                DORIS
Sometimes I think you ignore everything I try to teach you about life.

                GRACE
Not true. I listen to some of it. Just not the parts that make me cringe. Look, I am going to Exeter next year. We both want that, right? I'm very excited about starting, and that is all the more reason for me to do my best to ace the French exam tomorrow.

                DORIS
You are going to the reception, dear. This is an edict - not a debate.

                GRACE
Are you seriously going to force me to spend an evening with the waxworks - to hobnob with a bunch of blowhards and project the illusion of our perfect family?
                DORIS
Finally, you're getting it.

                GRACE
        (dropping her books on the table)

UUgghhh.

        (GRACE exits)

        (DORIS sips her champagne and give a wide smile of satisfaction)

        (BLACKOUT)

        (END OF SCENE)

ACT 1

Scene 2

SETTING: A living room or a simple table with three chairs

AT RISE: SUZANNE MAGEE and her daughter, MARLEEN, are seated and practicing for MARLEEN's French exam.

SUZANNE
She wants us to be at the party.

MARLEEN
Elle veut que nous soyons à la fête.

SUZANNE
Perfect. Sorry - parfait. Next one. You must know the truth.

MARLEEN
(straining)
Il faut que tu.... saverais la vérité.

SUZANNE
Mmmmm.

MARLEEN
I hate that verb!
(pauses, thinks)
I don't know. What is it?

SUZANNE
Il faut que tu...
(pauses, using encouraging hand gestures, hoping MARLEEN will get it, but MARLEEN does not respond)
...saches la vérité.

MARLEEN
Of course. Okay - one more.

SUZANNE
She would have done her homework, but she doesn't have any help.

MARLEEN
(thinking)
(delivered slowly)
Elle aurait fait son devoir, mais elle n'a pas d'assistance.

SUZANNE

Impressive. I think you're ready
for an A+.

                    MARLEEN
Not yet. I'm planning on getting up
early tomorrow for some last-minute
cramming.

                    SUZANNE
Whatever you think is best. Just be
sure to get enough sleep.

            (enter OWEN MAGEE,
            SUZANNE's husband and
            MARLEEN's father)

                    OWEN
You two are still at it?
            (to MARLEEN)
I'm surprised you don't have a beret
sprouting from your head and a
baguette growing from your armpit.
            (imitating Maurice
            Chevalier)
Huh, huh, huh.

                    MARLEEN
Stereotype much, dad? What's with
that "Huh, huh, huh" people do when
they want to bust on the French?
French people don't do that.

                    OWEN
They did in the old movies.

                    SUZANNE
               (sarcastically)

If it was in the old movies, then it must be true.

                MARLEEN
Don't encourage him, mom.

                SUZANNE
You're right. What's in the bag, Owen?

                OWEN
            (to MARLEEN)
I finally found the perfect suit for your graduation next week.

                SUZANNE
That's good news. We've been to every shop in town this week. Where'd you end up having success?

                OWEN
Marshall's. How convenient is that?! Half price always works better for me.

                MARLEEN
I would have gone there first. The clearance racks are the best.

                OWEN
I didn't have the clearance-rack luck. Suits are tough. I have yet to find a two-piece suit that actually fits. If the jacket fits, the trousers are huge, and if the

trousers fit, the jacket is too small.

MARLEEN
Ever occur to you that you might have FBS?

OWEN
What's that?

MARLEEN
Freakish body syndrome.

OWEN
That's not really a thing, is it?

MARLEEN
No, but for a second there, you were worried that it might be. Sorry.

OWEN
(to MARLEEN)
Sugar and spice and everything nice...yeah, right.

SUZANNE
She said she was sorry. Don't dwell, Owen. You are aware of the fact that tailors still exist, aren't you. Jackets and trousers can be easily altered.

OWEN
Yes, but if you can avoid them, you can be spared the agony of having a stranger with a mouthful of pins hold a tape measure up to your

crotch. Why pay for that if you don't have to?

                SUZANNE
I guess it's a moot point since you found one that fits.

                OWEN
It's almost like that.

                SUZANNE
What's that supposed to mean?

                OWEN
I tried on a couple of the suits. They looked good and the price was right, but same old, same old, so I had to do a little presto change-o in the fitting room.

                SUZANNE
           (in a shocked voice)
You didn't chance price tags, did you, OWEN?

                OWEN
I'm not a thief, Suzanne. I swapped the Orson Welles trousers for ones that fit and put them together with the jacket that fit. People must do it all the time; otherwise, suit parts wouldn't be so freakishly mismatched.

                MARLEEN
Like I said - FBS.

                SUZANNE

> (to OWEN)
> No, that's not a thing people do all the time. It's... well, it's not stealing, but it is dishonest. It's cheating... or... it's at least in the category of cheating.

MARLEEN
You probably could have just asked the salesperson. They are pretty down-to-earth in Marshall's.

SUZANNE
Marleen, men don't ask for directions, and they certainly don't ask for help when shopping. One of many gender flaws they possess.

MARLEEN
At least they're predictable. That's something, right?

OWEN
I figure whoever goes in to buy the next suit will try a few on and do exactly what I did. Eventually everybody gets a suit that fits, and the store makes a profit. It's a win-win.

SUZANNE

You're just trying to justify having done something illegal. Unethical. Not right... whatever the category is.

OWEN
I bet that right now another guy with FBS - a fat dude with narrow shoulders - is buying that combo I put together.

MARLEEN
Not worth an argument. There are worse things he could have done, Mom.

OWEN
Yes, there are.
    (to MARLEEN)
Like some of the things your mother does.
    (to SUZANNE)
You're not really one to judge about cheating, Suzanne. I saw the list of "interests" on your updated résumé, so don't get all self-righteous on me for buying a suit that actually fits.

SUZANNE
    (defensive)
A bit of embellishing is hardly cheating.

OWEN
A bit?! Deep sea diving! Are you serious? You won't even go outside when it's raining.

SUZANNE
I can be interested in something without ever having done it.

OWEN
And you think that's the assumption potential employers are going to make when they read that?

SUZANNE
They are free to assume what they like. It is not a lie.

MARLEEN
Technically, she's right, dad. As long as it's listed under interests and not accomplishments or hobbies, it's not cheating.

OWEN
Chalk this logic up to yet another gender difference.

SUZANNE
Look, if I were ever asked about it in an interview, I wouldn't lie.

OWEN
Do the two of you really think that switching suit parts is worse than misleading somebody who is thinking about hiring you?

MARLEEN
To me the suit thing and the résumé thing fall into the same category - white lies. They're innocent. Nobody gets hurt, nobody loses.

SUZANNE
Debatable.

OWEN

What is that "white lie" nonsense anyway. Is that some kind of race thing?

                    SUZANNE
Here we go. Another one of your sad segues, dear? When you want to change the subject, you just have to bring out the big guns, don't you?

                    MARLEEEN
He's never been known for his subtlety.

                    OWEN
Seriously, I have never heard of a black lie, have you?

                    SUZANNE
Where is this going, dear?

                    OWEN
If a lie isn't a white lie, then it must be a black one, right. We just don't add the color descriptor. Why not?

                    MARLEEN
I give up. Why not?

                    OWEN
Social injustice - that's why.
          (stands)
White things - good. Black things - bad. It's the kind of thinking we fought against all through the 70s. Unicorns - white. Darth Vader -

black. Angel food cake - white.
Devil's food cake - black. There's
a Black Death but not a white one.
Ever heard of white magic? I
haven't.

MARLEEN
Dad, you better never go to
Mississippi.

OWEN
Won't make my bucket list, trust me.

SUZANNE
Owen, please save the philosophical,
hippy tirade for our next evening
with the old gang.

OWEN
Fine, but at the end of the day, I
did not tell a white lie... or a
black lie... or a rainbow lie... or
a regular lie - I solved a problem.

SUZANNE
I'm not sure the Marshall's
employees would agree with that.

OWEN
Whatever. The conclusion is that we
both cheated. Me at Marshall's.
You with the résumé. Do we know
anybody who doesn't cheat? Anybody
who is completely honest about
everything?
(a pause. SUZANNE
contemplates the question)

MARLEEN
He's right, mom. Have you ever
checked your friends' profile pages
on Facebook? The ones on LinkedIn
are even worse. And these are good
people. Our friends. People list
awards and job titles that don't
even exist.

SUZANNE
   (looking up, contemplating
   and feeling guilty)
Sometimes, when I have friends over
for lunch, I always serve them cava
and tell them it's champagne. And I
did lie once - or should I say fib -
about the supposedly gluten-free,
vegan dessert I served. I couldn't
find free-range anything around
here.

MARLEEN
Cava and champagne are the same
thing - same ingredients, same
process - just made in different
places. Nobody notices the
difference, and as long as it has a
decent alcohol content, who cares?

OWEN
Just what every father of a teenage
daughter wants to hear.
SUZANNE

   (stands, becoming a bit
   manic and feeling guilty)

What, I'm supposed to drive half-way across the state to find ingredients to make people with probably-fabricated afflictions feel special? Nobody in developing countries has an I-can't-eat-that list. I am tired of first-world moaning.

                OWEN
At least we can agree on that. At age fifty, my sister reveals that she is lactose intolerant.

              MARLEEN
She made that up, because she got tired of waking up at five in the morning to help Uncle Edgar milk the cows.

              SUZANNE
His fault for letting her get away with it.

              OWEN
Probably afraid she'd sue him. It's even come to that – relatives suing each other. It's a mad, mad world.

              SUZANNE
Please don't use that expression, Owen. Makes you sound old.
              OWEN
I am. But at least people from my generation are honest about the important things.

              MARLEEN

Qualified honesty, dad? Really?
And you call yourself a former
hippie?

                    SUZANNE
We're beginning to beat a dead horse
here.

                    OWEN
And you say my expressions are old?!

                    MARLEEN
          (stands)
Let's wrap this up. I let my
friends believe what they want to
believe about me on social media.
Mom deceives her friends...

                    SUZANNE
I don't approve of your word choice.

                    MARLEEN
Mom omits certain factual details
when entertaining...

                    SUZANNE
Better.

                    MARLEEN
... and dad rearranges merchandise
to ensure customer satisfaction and
retail sales. Does that make us bad
people? Cheaters? Liars?

          SUZANNE   OWEN
It certainly does   It certainly
not.   Does not.

MARLEEN
Good. Settled.

OWEN
Forget the French, kiddo. You'd make a star lawyer.

SUZANNE
... or an excellent politician.

OWEN
An excellent oxymoron.

MARLEEN
(rolls her eyes; stands)
Now before I get back to my studies for tomorrow's exam, can we talk a little bit about my graduation?

SUZANNE
Of course we can. What's on your mind?

OWEN
All I can say is that I have the perfect suit for the occasion.

MARLEEN
We've moved on from that, Dad.

OWEN
Lawyer.

MARLEEN
It's about after the ceremony.

SUZANNE
We were thinking about inviting everybody to the buffet at the Peg-leg Parrot afterward... unless you want to have people back here. It's your day, so whatever you want.

MARLEEN
Buffets are gross. Cava, your gluten-free, organic quiches and a few batches of your vegan dim-sum would be awesome.

(BLACKOUT)

(END OF SCENE)

ACT 1

Scene 3

SETTING: Anywhere

AT RISE: Three schoolmates, LUCY, JANE and PAT are having an after-school discussion.

LUCY
Why does everything at this school have to have a theme?

Collaboration. Leadership.
Identity. Blah, blah, blah.

                    JANE
They are pretty important concepts,
and not all kids get to learn them
at home. We're lucky, because we
have normal parents.

                    LUCY
I guess, but it still feels like
they're trying to brainwash us.

                    PAT
Sometimes it does seem that way, but
I'm sure the education people mean
well.

                    LUCY
It's a little bit hypocritical
though, don't you think?

                    JANE
What do you mean?

                    LUCY
Take "collaboration," for example.
Everyone knows that Miss Davis and
Miss Gunderson can't stand each
other. Do they really think we
can't hear their cat fights in the
staff room?

                    PAT
I hope Miss Davis wins them. She's
cool.

                    LUCY
I'm sure she does. Gunderson's not
sharp enough to compete with her.
But that's not the point. The point
is that they preach these concepts
to us, but they don't always
practice them themselves.

                    JANE
They aren't robots, Lucy.

                    LUCY
I know, but it seems wrong that they
expect us to do things that they
aren't willing to do themselves.

                    PAT
Teachers kind of have to be like
that. It's their job to set
examples for us.

                    LUCY
But if they don't really mean what
they say, isn't that lying?

                    JANE
No. It's their job to try to guide
us in the right direction even if
that means sometimes saying things
that they don't necessarily believe.

                    PAT
Like what?

                    LUCY
Like Mr. Richardson. The law
requires him to teach Creationism

along with evolution in science class, and I happen to know for a fact that he is an atheist.

> PAT
>
> But that doesn't make him dishonest, does it?

> JANE
>
> Not at all. Teachers have a lot like in common with actors. Listen, just because Johnny Depp plays a gay, drunken, British pirate in the movies, doesn't mean he is one in real life. And it doesn't make him a liar - just mega rich... and a little bit hot… for an old guy.

> LUCY
>
> I see your point. It's just that it's sometimes a bit much. Even the school play has one of those themes.
>   (hands up, fingers moving.
>   Mocking the concept)
> Honesty!

> PAT   JANE
>
> We know. We're in it.

> LUCY
>
> Is it all preachy and boring?

> PAT
>
> Parts of it are, but most of it's okay.

> LUCY

Kids may have bought all of that talk about honesty before the Internet, but these days it's pretty easy for us to see how little of it there is in the world.

                JANE
That's true. Seems like a new scandal gets posted every second.

                LUCY
It almost seems as if there are more dishonest people than there are honest ones.

                JANE
Crooked politicians and crazy celebrities are one thing, but regular people like us at least try to be honest.

                LUCY
You can tell yourself that, but it isn't true. We are only honest when it's convenient.

                PAT
That sounds terrible.

                LUCY
Come on, Jane. Where did you tell your mother you were going after school yesterday?

                JANE

>   (a bit of defeat in her
>   voice, realizing PAT's
>   point)
To your house to study.

>   LUCY
And you were really...

>   JANE
In the park with Alex.

>   LUCY   PAT
>   (both teasing)
Ooooohhhh. Alex. In the park with Alex.

>   JANE
Real mature. Okay, I get it. You're a little bit right about the honesty thing. But if my parents don't like him, what else am I supposed to do?

>   LUCY
Exactly. I rest my case. We're honest when it suits us. You too, Pat. Last week, you told your mom that you didn't have any homework, because you wanted to go shopping with us... but you did have homework. How did that work out for you?

>   PAT
Teacher never checked it... and the shopping was way fun.

LUCY
And you regret having lied?

PAT
Actually, no.

LUCY
I didn't think so.

JANE
That's depressing.
LUCY
What's depressing?

JANE
The fact that you were right. We're honest only when it suits us.

LUCY
Save your drama for the play. It's human nature. You'll get used to it.

JANE
I'm sure your right... again.

(BLACKOUT)

(END OF SCENE)

<u>ACT I</u>

<u>Scene 4</u>

SETTING: Director PETERSON's office

AT RISE: PETERSON is sitting at his desk or at a simple table with his laptop.

PETERSON
Principal Gunderson, bring me the subsidies file, please, and an updated enrollment list.

(moments later, GUNDERSON enters with files and hands them to PETERSON)

PETERSON
Not the substitutes file – subsidies.

GUNDERSON
Oh. I thought they were the same thing
(starts to exit and then turns back)
Is that one word or two?
(PETERSON rolls his eyes at her)
Never mind. I'll find it.
(GUNDERSON exits)

PETERSON
(aside)
That woman may as well have been born headless. Of all the school districts in this state, we have to get stuck with the governor's niece.

GUNDERSON
(entering with another
file in her hand)
I think I found it.
PETERSON
Subcultures? Really? I repeat –
subsidies. Sub as in under. Sidies
as in... sounds like an urban place
where people live.
(GUNDERSON exits with the
file)
(aside)
Just three more years til
retirement. Three years. Three
very, very long and excruciating
years. Why oh why did I stop
drinking? What I could have been
drinki... uh, what could I have been
thinking?

GUNDERSON
(enters with yet another
file)
This has to be the one. See.
(pointing to the tab on
the file)
It has that word on it that looks
like the one you said.
(PETERSON takes the file
and looks at it)

PETERSON
Yeah. That's the one. Now please
take a seat.
(looks through the file)
We're at a pivotal moment here in
the district.

                    GUNDERSON
That sure sounds like an important
kind of moment.

                    PETERSON
As I said - pivotal.

                    GUNDERSON
Yes. Very pivial. More pivial than
most, I bet.

                    PETERSON
          (rolling his eyes again)
We have an opportunity to increase
district funding by almost fifty
percent.

                    GUNDERSON
Opportunities can be really good. I
like them.

                    PETERSON
Please try to keep your observations
to a minimum. I left my blood
pressure meds in the car.

                    GUNDERSON
Got it. Nobody likes pressure. It
usually means there's more work to
do, and who wants that?

                    PETERSON
Right. Our demographics need to be
updated immediately. Patterns
indicate a significant influx of
ethnic minorities into the district,
and I need the most recent figures.

GUNDERSON
Democratics. Reflux. Figures. Got it.

PETERSON
Do you?

GUNDERSON
I know it sounds important.

PETERSON
(exaggerated and slow)
You have no idea.

GUNDERSON
You'd be surprised how often I get that.

PETERSON
(shaking head from side to side)
No. No. I really wouldn't. Can you print out a current enrollment list with admission dates and students' countries of origin?

GUNDERSON
(with a condescending giggle)
Mr. Director, I'm not a magician. If I had those kinds of powers, I'd be headlining in Las Vegas. Do you have any reasonable requests?

PETERSON

I do. Send in Miss Morris and then
go do some shopping at the lost and
found table. That's one of your
things, right?

                    GUNDERSON
Now you're getting it.
          (exits and MISS MORRIS
          enters)

                    MORRIS
I know already. I was
eavesdropping. The entertainment
value around here could give Netflix
a run for its money.

                    PETERSON
How do you work with that woman?

                    MORRIS
Nobody actually works **WITH** her.
More like around her. If she isn't
moving plants and chairs around,
she's devouring everything that
shows up in the staff room.
          (hands PETERSON some
          files)
Here's the data you were trying to
get the magician to print out. I
added a bunch of recent MAP scores
to it this morning, so it's
completely up to date.

                    PETERSON
You do your job and then some while
the resident magician does nothing
and collects double your salary.
That must really bother you.

MORRIS
It's not so bad. I'm used to it.
Been in the district for decades.
Sometimes I feel like a dinosaur,
though. You know that the new,
young ones refer to me as an
"amateur," right? And why? Because
I think people should just do their
jobs without requiring a fleet of
assistants or consultants.

PETERSON
Sorry, amateur, they call them
"critical friends" these days. The
word *consultant* has too many
negative connotations.

MORRIS
And "critical friend" doesn't?
Sorry. I don't buy into the ever-
devolving jargon. Too old school, I
guess.

PETERSON
Old school works for me, Morris.
          (looking at the files)
As far as I'm concerned, you're
worth every cent you're not being
paid.

MORRIS
Gee, thanks.

PETERSON
          (holding up papers)
This is exactly what we need to get
started.

MORRIS
Started on what?

PETERSON
The state department of education just passed a new piece of legislation that offers a significant boost in funding to schools with large immigrant populations.

MORRIS
That's us.
        (she sits)

PETERSON
We qualify if at least twenty percent of our students have immigrated into the country in the last five years.

MORRIS
EAL classes are bursting at the seams, and lots of parents need translators at conferences, so let's go for it. How much extra funding are we talking?

PETERSON
Enough to bring back the music and arts programs and then some. We're talking seven figures here.

MORRIS
Per year?

PETERSON
Per year.

MORRIS
Ready to do some math?
> (PETERSON and MORRIS look through the papers and work on adding up the numbers. As they do so, they converse.)

PETERSON
Geez, you think we have enough Smiths, Davidsons and Gallaghers?

MORRIS
Original settlers are still going strong in these parts.

PETERSON
Fourteen Gutiérrez kids and twenty-two Gonzalez kids? Really?

MORRIS
Mexico isn't all margaritas and quesadillas, Joe. Outside of Cancun, it can get pretty rough.
> (still calculating, short pause)

Okay. I have my totals. You?

PETERSON
Yep.
> (MORRIS hands him a paper, which he peruses. He pounds his fist on the desk.)

Shitake mushrooms! We're two kids short.

MORRIS
We're sure to get a few more once school starts again.

PETERSON
That won't help us. Apps have to be submitted by the end of the month.

MORRIS
Not much we can do then. We tried. At least you keep yourself informed about what kind of extra help is out there. I know I appreciate that. So we try again next semester.

PETERSON
Unless...

MORRIS
Unless what? We recruit a couple of refugees?

PETERSON
Last director tried that, and we know how that worked out. Leaves too obvious a paper trail. We could, however, cook the books a little. Apply a little creativity to our database.

MORRIS
You're joking, right?

PETERSON

Do I look like I'm joking?

			MORRIS
You are aware of the nearly extinct concept of ethics, aren't you?

			PETERSON
Ethics aren't becoming extinct - just more malleable. Today more than ever, truth is relative, abstract even. Things that may seem to be wrong may actually not be, because they ultimately result in a bigger right.

			MORRIS
Who are you trying to convince? Me or yourself? An example of your theory might help.

			PETERSON
Do you have any idea how many countries are currently violating the Geneva Convention in order to supply arms to people fighting whacky extremists around the world?

			MORRIS
I'm well aware of the blurred lines and the vortex of legal loopholes, but we are not a world power. We're a school, and the law is the law.

			PETERSON
Only if we get caught.

			MORRIS

Not sure I'm liking the "we" part of this anymore.

                    PETERSON
State inspectors rarely make visits, and even when they do, they only skim the paperwork. Nobody wants to die of boredom.

                    MORRIS
And if it doesn't get past them?

                    PETERSON
Technical errors. Blame it on the damned auto-correct. Last week I sent out a text comment on a social media photo. An old friend. I meant to write, "You look like a pro," but auto-correct somehow turned it into, "You look like a bro."

                    MORRIS
So what? Still sounds okay.

                    PETERSON
I got sixteen comments about racial profiling!

                    MORRIS
Ouch. That's different.

                    PETERSON
Why shouldn't we take advantage of the glitches in computer programs. They screw up all the time. Wouldn't it be worth the risk to get

art and music back? The greater good?

                    MORRIS
The end justifies the means. I get it.

                    PETERSON
Exactly.

                    MORRIS
What kind of intentional glitches were you thinking about?

                    PETERSON
          (looks at papers)
For example, take this Alicia Lipp. What kind of name is that? Clearly it's a shortened version of something more ethnic.

                    MORRIS
Right. Like Lippenstein.

                    PETERSON
That just sounds scary.

                    MORRIS
Visions of Donatella Versace, right.

                    PETERSON
          (cringes at the conjured
      image)
That's the one.
          (concentrating)
Lippinski! Eastern European. Scary stuff happening in the Ukraine these

days... why wouldn't the Lippinski family come here? They would.

> MORRIS

So the Lippinskis escape to the West to make a better life for Alicia. I'm following.

> PETERSON

The admission date is within the range. We just add a few letters to the last name and change Kansas to Kiev.

> MORRIS

I don't know how Kansas is gonna feel about that.

> PETERSON
> (looking through lists)

And this Nicholas Dilk. Dilk sounds more like an acronym than an actual name.

> MORRIS

It is. I heard it on a sit-com. Stands for: "Dad I'd Like to ..." Never mind.

> PETERSON

Then we'd be doing little Nicky a favor by changing it.

> MORRIS

Tempting to go Eastern European again with that one.

                    (shrugs shoulders)
    Dilkinski?

                    PETERSON
                    (thinking)
Too close to Lippinski. Originality
needed here.
                    (thinking)
Let's go South African...
Dilkhoffer.

                    MORRIS
As fun as this creative little
exercise may be, we are so getting
into big trouble. And tenure won't
help us.

                    PETERSON
Not if nobody finds out. We'll be
the only two who know. Besides, the
extra funding could also result in
some well-deserved and overdue
salary increases.

                    MORRIS
The "we" is starting to sound
better.

                    PETERSON
Not even the hint of a word about
this to anyone.

                    MORRIS
Wild Turkey couldn't drag it out of
me.

                    PETERSON
You mean wild horses.

                    MORRIS
You have your drink. I have mine.

                    (BLACKOUT)

                    (END OF SCENE)

                    ACT 1

                    Scene 5

SETTING: Exam room consisting
                    of two or more desks
                    far enough apart from
                    each other for actors
                    to easily walk the
                    imagined aisle.

AT RISE: GRACE and MARLEEN sit
                    at desks. Principal
                    GUNDERSON is in the
                    room holding test
                    papers and pencils.

                    GUNDERSON
               (reading from manual)
You are here for the Universal
Baccalaureate French examination.
If this is not the course for which
you are meant to be testing, please
indicate this to the exam proctor
slash invigilator now.
               (looking up and seeing no
                reaction from the
                girls)

The proctor slash invigilator will now distribute test booklets and answer sheets. Do not open or touch them until instructed to do so.
   (distributes papers)
Before you begin, make sure that you have left all electronic devices and subject materials outside of the testing room. The presence of any of these items in this room may result in the invalidation of this exam.
   (looks at students who nod
   in agreement)
You have ninety minutes to complete the exam, and you will be given a thirty-minute and a five-minute warning. Open your exams and begin.
   (they open exam booklets
  and begin but GUNDERSON
  continues reading)
Note to proctor slash invigilator: remain focused on students at all times. Your movements around the examination room should be minimal...
   (students look at each
   other, confused)
... as they may cause distractions. You may not read or...

MARLEEN
Principal, Gunderson, I think that part is for you to read to yourself. The exam has already begun.

GUNDERSON

Silence. No speaking during the exam, young lady.

> (ticking clock sound effect begins. Students read and write. Both are serious and engaged. GUNDERSON walks up and down the center aisle. Every now and again, she whips her head toward the students to try to catch them cheating. They react with grimaces that clearly indicate their irritation with her. Each time GUNDERSON walks down the aisle, away from the girls, she takes out her phone and scrolls through her Facebook feed. When she walks up the aisle, toward the girls, she conceals the phone. When checking Facebook, she occasionally grunts, giggles or lets out a "hhmm." When GUNDERSON releases utterances, the students turn to the center aisle to look at her. They are visibly annoyed.)

GUNDERSON
Eyes on your own papers.

> (GUNDERSON continues with her phone routine.
> GRACE becomes fidgety and appears to be struggling, as she is unprepared. She tries to look at MARLEEN's paper and MARLEEN covers hers. Next time GUNDERSON walks down the exam aisle, GRACE mouths the word, "Please" to MARLEEN. She is desperate. MARLEEN softens and slides her paper to the edge of her desk closest to GRACE. GUNDERSON turns around and witnesses this.

GUNDERSON
That is NOT in the instruction manual! Exam compromised. Exam over!

> (GUNDERSON collects the papers)

MARLEEN
Wait. I'm not finished.

GUNDERSON
Oh, but you are. I am in charge here. I know what I saw. And I am missing a free breakfast in the staff room as we speak.

GRACE
I focus better when I look up and stare away from my paper.

GUNDERSON
That doesn't even make sense. Do you really think I am as stupid as I look?
> (no response, an uncomfortable pause)

Had you responded differently, I may have reconsidered.
> (she leaves with the papers)

GRACE
I'm sorry...

MARLEEN
Marleen.

GRACE
Marleen. I didn't mean to... I didn't think she'd... have a clue. Does she?

MARLEEN
My parents are going to be so disappointed. And furious.

GRACE
Mine will go into full-throttle lecture mode. Even though it's their fault I got no study time in last night... or sleep.

MARLEEN
How can your parents possibly control things like that?

                    GRACE
Have you met them?

          (announcement over the
          school speaker system from
          GUNDERSON)

               GUNDERSON'S VOICE
Grace Jenkins and Marleen Magee,
report to the director's office
immediately.

                   MARLEEN
Great.

                    GRACE
Don't worry. They have nothing on
us. You didn't do anything wrong.
Actually, neither did I... never got
the chance to. Come on. Let's get
this over with.

                   MARLEEN
I think I may have to puke first.
          (the girls race off stage)

               (BLACKOUT)

               (END OF SCENE)

INTERVAL/INTERMISSION

ACT II

Scene 1

SETTING: Director PETERSON's office

AT RISE: PETERSON and GUNDERSON converse

PETERSON
What were you thinking, Gunderson?! Now we have to scrap an exam and report this to the U.B. Any idea how this is going to look? There goes my bonus and possibly the school's reputation... not to mention the state funding we are up for.

GUNDERSON
But they were cheating.

PETERSON
How can you be sure? How is that even possible? You supervise an exam with only two students in it, and you can't even do that right?

GUNDERSON
In my defense, I was never sent on a proctor slash invigilator's training course even though I applied for one last year.

PETERSON
Yes, I recall that application. Two weeks in Miami... in January. You are just SO dedicated to education, aren't you?

GUNDERSON

I couldn't go to the local training thing because of my foot operation.

            PETERSON
Yeah, you have a lot of those, don't you? What's wrong with it anyway? Keeps getting caught in your mouth?

            GUNDERSON
I don't even know what that means, but I'm sure it was meant to be funny or mean.

            PETERSON
I will not allow your incompetence to compromise the reputation of our school. You need to make this situation go away.

            GUNDERSON
Too late. I already called the parents, and they are on their way here as I speak... or as you do... or as we both do.

            PETERSON
And who authorized that?

            GUNDERSON
                (smugly)
It's procedure. I read it in the handbook.

            PETERSON
You read the handbook, but you can't read a simple exam protocol manual

unless it is put in front of you in Miami next to a mojito?

GUNDERSON
Why would anybody put a manual next to a mojito? Everybody knows those people can't read English.

PETERSON
(aside, to audience)
Three more years. Long, long, long years.
(GRACE and MARLEEN enter)
Have a seat, ladies.
(they sit)
Care to explain yourselves?
(enter QUINCY, DORIS [with champagne], OWEN [with briefcase] and SUZANNE)

DORIS
Why on earth have you called us in here?!

PETERSON
Mr. and Mrs. Jenkins, Mr. and Mrs. Magee, thank you for coming in. Please have a seat. Anybody for a coffee?

DORIS
(hoisting her champagne)
I brought my own thank you very much.

QUINCY
I wouldn't mind one if you have something in that desk of yours to enhance it.

PETERSON
This is a school, Mr. Jenkins.
Alcohol is strictly forbidden.

QUINCY
Then you better get my wife's
bloodstream out of here.

DORIS
(sarcastic and dismissive)
Your humor, much like your oblivion
to my gorgeousness, escapes me.

GUNDERSON
Not to worry, Mr. Jenkins. We have
a few bottles we confiscated from
school dances. How about a nice
orange brandy from Serbia?

PETERSON
(to GUNDERSON)
Is it even remotely possible for you
to keep that foot someplace other
than in your mouth?!

QUINCY
Orange brandy? How vulgar... but it
beats milk and sugar.

OWEN
We're fine, Mr. Peterson.

SUZANNE
We just want to know what's going
on.
(GUNDERSON exits and
returns in a few seconds
with a coffee for QUINCY)

> (to MARLEEN)
> You didn't get into a fight, did you, dear?

MARLEEN
No, nothing like that.

PETERSON
Principal Gunderson seems to think that the girl's were cheating on today's French exam.

DORIS
Cheating! We don't do that in our family. Our ancestors were first-class passengers on the *Mayflower* for your information.

OWEN
Ours arrived here on the Greyhound, but Marleen doesn't cheat either.

SUZANNE
Because she doesn't have to.

PETERSON
Everybody just calm down and let's hear from the girls.
> (to GRACE and MARLEEN)
> So what exactly happened in the exam room?

GRACE
The exam room was boiling hot, and it was hard to concentrate. And I was really tired... and the exam questions were confusing.

DORIS
Not for somebody as bright as you, dear.

QUINCY
There must be more to this, Grace. You are a Jenkins. A natural talent.

MARLEEN
It's true. It was really hot in there.

GUNDERSON
We are not here to talk about the weather.
    (points at GRACE)
I witnessed you looking at her paper. And you...
    (points at MARLEEN)
were not making it very difficult.

QUINCY
Trust me, Principal Gunderson, our daughter is the product of a very strong gene pool, and she does not need to cheat.

GUNDERSON
Please do not change the subject. The pool has nothing to do with this. That's a P.E. issue.

QUINCY
Indeed. Sounds like somebody's gene pool might benefit from a bit of chlorine.
    (stares at GUNDERSON)

DORIS
(taking out phone)
I think I may need to record this meeting. Accusations of this nature have legal consequences.

PETERSON
There is really no need for that, Mrs. Jenkins.
(to MARLEEN)
Tell us more, Marleen.

MARLEEN
(looking at GRACE)
I was thinking about the answers and trying to concentrate. Maybe I lost track of where my paper was, but I don't think Grace was trying to...

DORIS
Infernally hot. Difficult to concentrate. Sounds very stressful to me. You are aware, Director Peterson, of the effect that extreme heat has on one's ability to concentration.

PETERSON
Indeed I am, Mrs. Jenkins, but the fact remains that...

GUNDERSON
The fact remains that the girls were caught cheating.

PETERSON

>   (gritting his teeth)
> I'm handling this, Principal
> Gunderson.

>   DORIS
> And what if our Grace simply has
> problems concentrating? Is that a
> crime?

>   GRACE
> I do not have a problem
> concentrating. Well, no more than
> anybody else does. I just choose to
> ignore a lot of things that aren't
> worth paying attention to.
>   (looks at her mother and
>   grimaces)
> But it was as hot as Hades in there.

>   GUNDERSON
> Language, young lady!

>   GRACE
> It's a literary allusion to Greek
> mythology, Principal Gunderson.

>   GUNDERSON
> If you are having literal illusions,
> then there is a whole different
> protocol we need to follow here.
>   (PETERSON shoots her a
>   menacing look)

>   SUZANNE
> This conversation is becoming as
> stressful as any exam room I've ever
> been in. Please tell us why are we

here. What does this have to do
with Marleen? What did she do?

> PETERSON

I apologize for the digression, Mrs.
Magee.
> > (to Marleen)

Marleen, can you shed some light on
the situation? What happened in
there?

> MARLEEN
> > (nervous)

We were writing and trying to
ignore the sweat running down our
faces. I didn't mean to... It
wasn't like I planned to...

> GUNDERSON

To what? Cheat? If anybody is an
expert on cheating, it's me, and I
know what I saw.
> > (to MARLEEN)

You're saying your paper
accidentally drifted to the far end
of your desk, so your friend here
could copy it?

> OWEN

Sorry, but that just does not sound
like Marleen.

> GUNDERSON

Mr. Magee, I am an experienced
proctor slash invigilator; if I say
something happened, it did.

> SUZANNE

But isn't it possible that there is some sort of misunderstanding? Marleen was truly ready for that exam. We reviewed together for hours last night.

              DORIS
We did the same.
         (GRACE shoots DORIS a
         look)

            PETERSON
We are not really getting anywhere here. I have a suggestion...

              DORIS
I have one too. These schools all have security cameras.
         (stands)
I demand to see the footage from the exam room. I will not allow my daughter to be labeled as a cheater.

              GRACE
That might not be the best idea, mom.

              DORIS
Nonsense. No child of mine will end up with a sullied reputation as a result of somebody else's incompetence.

            PETERSON
Girls, why don't you wait for us in the hallway. We'll call you back in if we need you.
         (the two students exit)

GUNDERSON
We have security cameras here?

PETERSON
Mrs. Jenkins, I assure you that we offer a top-notch program here. Let's try to keep things positive and professional.
> (begins pacing nervously behind them)

QUINCY
For once, my wife is making some sense. Let's see the footage.

OWEN
Yes, why not take advantage of our *Brave New World*? Cameras don't lie, right?

DORIS
They certainly seem to lie a helluva lot when I am on the beach in a bikini.

QUINCY
Can you please spare us the imagery?!

> (DORIS shoots QUINCY a look)

SUZANNE
I think checking the security camera footage is a wonderful idea. I know my daughter, and she truly struggles with dishonesty.

>   (looks at OWEN)
> We are proud of her for that - among other things.

DORIS
Are you implying that this is Grace's fault? That she cheated? *Mayflower* trumps Greyhound every time, my dear.

SUZANNE
I am implying no such thing. And you wasted a perfectly pompous - and sad - insult on me. Truly educated people know exactly what the passengers of the *Mayflower* were like - and what they did when they got here.

DORIS
Yes, we do. They produced us.

OWEN
(to DORIS)
I think you just made my wife's point for her.

QUINCY
This meeting has already lasted too long, and it's solving nothing. I have pressing business matters to deal with. Can we please move on?

SUZANNE
The security camera footage, Director Peterson. If you don't comply, you better hope Johnny Cochran is still available for work.

PETERSON
No need for threats. Principal
Gunderson and I will check the video
footage and be back pronto.
> (PETERSON grabs GUNDERSON
> by the arm and they
exit)

DORIS
> (pulling a small champagne
> bottle from her purse
> and refilling her glass)
Good Lord, spending time with school
people is about as interesting as
watching paint dry. Can this please
be over soon. I'm sure I'm missing
an important lunch somewhere.

SUZANNE
We have things to do too, but it is
important for us to be here for the
girls.
> (to QUINCY and SUZANNE)
We never did get the chance to meet
properly. Sorry. I'm Suzanne.

> (OWEN, SUZANNE, QUINCY and
> DORIS exchange
introductions)

OWEN
That's more like it. Come on, guys
- we're here for the kids. Let's
count our blessings that we are
meeting in a school and not in a
police station.

DORIS
(easily distracted from
the conversation)
How do they manage to get all
schools to smell exactly the same?

QUINCY
Don't change the subject or we'll be
here that much longer.

SUZANNE
All kids do dumb things at school at
some point. It's almost a rite of
passage. We've all been there. This
will be settled and forgotten in a
few weeks.

QUINCY
(takes phone out and looks
at it, begins texting)
Sooner would be good.

DORIS
(to OWEN and SUZANNE)
You're right, of course. Sorry. I
am very stressed. It's just that we
set such high standards for Grace -
because of our background - and this
kind of thing is upsetting.

SUZANNE
(a bit defensive)
We set high standards for Marleen
too.

QUINCY

Of course you do. Why wouldn't you? You want her to have better lives than you do, obviously.

OWEN
Obviously?

DORIS
Well, you know. Family heritage.

OWEN
Seriously?

SUZANNE
Just let it go, Owen.

OWEN
I'm not sure I like where this meeting is going.

DORIS
Nonsense. It's going fine. And even better since that dippy principal is gone.
(giving a cougaresque look)
Though Director Peterson might warrant some closer examination.

QUINCY
(still texting)
Please, feel free to examine away!

SUZANNE
This is probably just a big nothing. Our girls, after all, are honest.

DORIS
Yes, honest. Integrity is key in our family.

QUINCY
(still texting)
Honesty and integrity. Yes.

OWEN
Enough about families and heritages. Let's change the subject.

SUZANNE
No politics, Owen!

OWEN
Right.
(to QUINCY)
You're on that phone an awful lot. You're not a reporter, are you?

QUINCY
(puts phone away)
No. Stock market. This phone is my office.

SUZANNE
That is so exciting! I see the big wigs ringing the bell sometimes on CNN. Our lives aren't as glamorous as all that.

QUINCY

I've never been anywhere near the bell. And the glamour part is highly overrated.

DORIS
Glamour cannot be overrated!

OWEN
I have a plumbing business here in the city...

SUZANNE
... which does very well.

DORIS
I'm sure it does.

OWEN
I like it because it's honest work.

QUINCY
Is it really?

SUZANNE
What do you mean by that?

QUINCY
It's just that last time our toilet was stopped up during the night, the guy who came to fix it charged us three times the day rate.

OWEN
That's pretty standard fare. Night rates are just higher. Inconvenient time to head out.

QUINCY
A job is a job and a price is a price, right?

OWEN
Depends. What if one of your stock market people called you at two in the morning to meet downtown for a transaction? Shouldn't your commission be more, because you had to get up in the middle of the night?

QUINCY
Stock market bell rings at four. There are no deals at two in the morning.

OWEN
Plumbing doesn't follow the market schedule. If I do get a call at two in the morning to fix a toilet, I have to get up and dressed and leave my family. I think it's fair to charge more for that than for a toilet that decides to malfunction between nine and five. You market guys are lucky - a full night's sleep is a luxury I don't have.

QUINCY
You chose a job that has round-the-clock possibilities. I chose one that doesn't. I don't see why the rates should change after the sun goes down. A service is a service.

OWEN
Your work must be a little bit like that too. Surely you get the odd after-hours tip that boosts the next day's profit.

DORIS
(defensive)
We have no idea what you are talking about.

OWEN
But if some big financial changes happen even after the bell rings, you don't just go to bed and wait for the next bell to ring at nine the next morning. You act on them somehow, right?

QUINCY
That would be illegal.

OWEN
Come on. Wall Street isn't exactly known for its honesty.

QUINCY
Neither are plumbers who overcharge.

OWEN
I'm not judging, just making observations.

DORIS
You two are giving me a headache.

QUINCY
Sure it isn't your "coffee," dear?

(DORIS shoots QUINCY a
dirty look)

SUZANNE
We're getting too serious here.

OWEN
Suzanne is right. In the end, we all do what we have to do to make a decent living. We take advantage of profitable opportunities.

QUINCY
Is there any other way?

DORIS
(sipping champagne)
Can we leave yet?

(BLACKOUT)

(END OF SCENE)

ACT II

Scene 2

SETTING: In an office or at a simple table

AT RISE: GUNDERSON and PETERSON are in a discussion after having viewed the security footage.

PETERSON
What could you have been thinking, Gunderson?! Are you a complete buffoon?

GUNDERSON
How was I supposed to know that the phone thing applied to staff too? I'm not one of the Fantastic Four.

PETERSON
No, you most definitely are not.

GUNDERSON
(mistaking the insult for a compliment)
Thank you.

PETERSON
(rolls eyes)
Thanks to you and your Facebook frenzy during the exam, we cannot show those families this footage. Any bright solutions you care to dazzle me with?

GUNDERSON
Do I need to remind you that you are the director? I don't get paid to make important decisions.

PETERSON
You shouldn't get paid at all. You're about as useless as sunscreen in the Netherlands.
(simile can be adapted to performance location)

GUNDERSON
I really don't care what you say to those parents, but those girls are not getting a re-take. I saw them cheat.

PETERSON
You compromised the exam, so you really don't have much say in this matter. The girls will get a re-take.

GUNDERSON
We don't have to give them one if we don't show the security video. I'll look like a fool. What happened to sticking together?

PETERSON
Sticking together with you just means covering up one of your blunders after another, and I am pretty much over that. Might be time for Uncle Governor to find you a job you can actually do.
> (pause)

And quite frankly, Gunderson, he has a better chance of finding the Holy Grail.
> (pause)

We are not showing the security footage. Discussion over.
> (to audience)

Why am I even having a conversation with somebody who makes Adam Sandler look like a nuclear physicist?

GUNDERSON
(giggling)
He's funny.

PETERSON
(obviously fed up with her
nonsense and pointing
in her face)
Here's how this is gonna go down, Gunderson. First of all, you say nothing when we go back in there. I'll do the talking.

GUNDERSON
Your tone is not helping me to like you.

PETERSON
Like me?! That's the last thing I want.

GUNDERSON
(confused)
Then we're on the same page.
(vacuous, clueless smile)
I like you too.

PETERSON
(shaking his head and
ignoring her last remark)
In addition to capturing you Facebooking and playing Candy Crush during a UB exam, the security camera recorded the temperature of the room... luckily for you.

GUNDERSON

You changed the subject to weather, and I'm supposed to be the dumb one?!

             PETERSON
Trust me – you are. My garden tools could do your job. Luckily for you, the temperature in the testing room was five degrees hotter than the maximum mandated by the district.

             GUNDERSON
We did that all the time as students. Held cigarette lighters under the thermostats to get early dismissals. Teachers did it even more than we did.

             PETERSON
A partial explanation for why you know what you know.
        (pauses in frustration)
Please stop giving me irresistible opportunities to insult you – it's too easy. Just listen. We go back in there, apologize for the administrative oversight of the state temperature regulation and schedule a re-take with the girls.

             GUNDERSON
But then I look like an idiot.

             PETERSON
What, you haven't seen a mirror yet?

             GUNDERSON

I am not intimidated by you and your real credentials. You do know who my uncle is, don't you.

PETERSON
I do indeed. He's the one who passed the legislation requiring us to dismiss students immediately if classroom temperatures go above your IQ. Oh, sorry - then we'd have to turn the heat on, wouldn't we.

(BLACKOUT)

(END OF SCENE)

ACT II

Epilogue

SETTING: A bare stage/space

AT RISE: All cast members stand frozen in an open space. When a spotlight illuminates a couple and/or individual, the illuminated

actor(s) come to life and speak.
(spot on GRACE and MARLEEN)

MARLEEN

Grace received a six in the end.

GRACE
And MARLEEN pulled off a perfect seven.

MARLEEN
People say that things happen for a reason...

GRACE
... which I usually think is their justification for having to accept results they never really wanted or anticipated.

MARLEEN
But not in this case. Grace got the time she needed to prepare for the exam, and we had an entire day to study together.

GRACE
It was a win-win... more of a win for me, because Marleen didn't really need that.

MARLEEN
It didn't hurt. Probably made the difference between a six and a seven.

GRACE
I didn't have to cheat. I aced that thing all on my own, and trust me - Gunderson was watching us like Honey Boo watches Paula Dean eat butter.

MARLEEN

In a way, I am glad we were caught.
It forced us both to prove what we
know and what we are capable of.

GRACE
Gunderson is livid that we did so
well.

MARLEEN
Of course she is - she came so close
to exposing her incompetence.

GRACE
She didn't need our help for that.

MARLEEN
Maybe it's not her fault that she
thinks Belgium is in France. Maybe
we are just luckier than she is.
Clearly, she is resentful that we
are...

GRACE   MARLEEN
...the poster children for
potential.
          (the girls give each other
a high five)

MARLEEN
I feel sorry for her.

GRACE
You're just too nice.

MARLEEN

Maybe I am, but I like that about myself.
>   (spot off of GRACE and MARLEEN and up on OWEN and SUZANNE)

OWEN

I have to hand it to that Quincy. He made me think. I decided to try charging the same rates at night as I do for day, and the business is pouring in. No plumber pun intended.

SUZANNE
> (to audience)

He had to hire six more employees.

OWEN
> (enthusiastically)

I created six new jobs for people, and my profit margin is stronger than ever.

SUZANNE

Now we can afford to let Marleen go to any university she wants to.
>   (to the audience)

She's been accepted at Chapel Hill, Vassar, New York University - even Drew.

OWEN
> (disdainfully)

Yeah, but Drew is in New Jersey.

SUZANNE

(defensively)
Meryl Streep and Bruce Springstein come from there. And Princeton is there; how bad could it be?

OWEN

Ever been to Newark?
(spot off of OWEN and
SUZANNE and up on QUINCY)

QUINCY

I'm going to jail next week. Minimum security, so I still have Internet, cable and a gym.
(to the audience)
Never trust a blabbermouth broker.
(pauses, thinks)
Maybe I can turn this into something lucrative and get the big bucks rolling in again. A manly version of *Orange is the New Black*.
(realizes what he said and cringes)
On second thought... not so interested in meeting Big Bubba.
(spot off of QUINCY and up on DORIS)

DORIS

(to the audience)
I tried to warn him and you are my witnesses. I don't feel guilty at all. Well, maybe a little bit. He did provide the surgical life-style to which I have become accustomed. And I do look good, right?
(hopefully a reaction from the audience)

I can deal with this. I am a strong woman. A fierce woman. I have no fear of flying... my mother, myself... I am woman, hear me roar.
> (puckering up and giving a mild shimmy)

A sensual woman who has been deprived for far too long.
> (a bit distraught, to audience)

Am I just being selfish?
> (back to sensual)

Yes. I deserve selfish. I still have a lot of mileage in me, and I did not go through the agony of lifts and tucks not to have them noticed, right?
> (she pauses and thinks)

Quincy will be out in less than two years. It'll give him time to think... and learn to appreciate me.
> (pauses)

In the meantime, I it might be fun to flirt a little. Test the market. What Quincy doesn't know, won't hurt him.
> (dramatic pause)

Maybe some time in the big house will make him appreciate the most important thing he's had all along. ME!
> (spot off of DORIS and up on MORRIS)

MORRIS

Sometimes one has to be grateful to South American dictators. Three new refugee families arrived in the

district last week. They were a
deus ex machina for Peterson and me.
>   (pause)

I was prepared to press enter on the
Lipp and Dilk changes. And without a
twinge of guilt... or so I tell
myself now. That really isn't me,
but to get art and music back in
this place, I would have definitely
compromised the district's sacred UB
learner profile characteristics.
Sometimes doing the right thing is
really just wrong.
>   (to the audience)

You get that, right?
>   (back into character)

Those programs are back now and
thriving, and the students are
happier than ever. I have no
problem sleeping at night. My
conscience and I are BFFs.
>   (spot off of MORRIS and up
>   on PETERSON)

PETERSON

Morris and I lucked out. Yes, we
were prepared to fudge the records
to make things better here for
everybody, but fate intervened and
we didn't have to.
>   (pause)

I decided to leave while at the top
of my game. Three more years here
may have killed me... and I would
have missed out on retirement.
>   (dreamily)

Happy hour every evening.
>   (focused again)

Mojitos are awesome, by the way – whether they can read English or not. I've never been happier. And don't even get me started about the early-bird specials!
>(to the audience)

While you are still in the work force... or as my new retired self refers to it – the work farce – make sure you take care of the good ones. The ones who work hard. The ones who give more than they take. The ones who care. Supporting them and leaving them as your legacy might be the best thing you can do to make this complicated planet work. Just so you know, I promoted Morris before I quit.
>(smile and thumbs up to the audience)
>(spot off PETERSON and up on GUNDERSON)

GUNDERSON
>(with arrogance and condescension)

Naturally, I am the one to have the final word at this important meeting.
>(pauses, looks confused)

However, I have forgotten my lines.
>(spot off. Full cast assembles on stage)
>(lights up on full cast)

ONE OR MORE CAST MEMBERS

"... before I can live with other folks, I've got to live with myself.
	(pause)
The one thing that doesn't abide by majority rule is a person's conscience."
	(pause)
Harper Lee via Atticus Finch.

		(BLACKOUT)

		THE END

www.ingramcontent.com/pod-product-compliance
Lightning Source LLC
Chambersburg PA
CBHW070544300426
44113CB00011B/1793